WE ARE ALL WEIRD

WE ARE ALL WEIRD
THE MYTH OF MASS AND THE END OF COMPLIANCE

BY SETH GODIN

THE
DOMINO
PROJECT
POWERED BY amazon.com

© 2011 Do You Zoom, Inc.

The Domino Project

Published by Do You Zoom, Inc.

The Domino Project is powered by Amazon. Sign up for updates and free stuff at www.thedominoproject.com.

This is the first edition. If you'd like to suggest a riff for a future edition, please visit our website.

Godin, Seth, 1960—

We Are All Weird: The myth of mass and the end of compliance / Seth Godin

p. cm.

ISBN 978-1-936719-22-8

Printed in the United States of America

WE ARE ALL WEIRD

INTRODUCTION:
THE PREGNANT ELEPHANT

Ad legend Linda Kaplan Thaler tells the story of a zoo in Belgium, down on its luck. The crowds had stopped coming.

With the emergence of so many alternative amusements, diversions and novelties, the zoo had fallen on hard times. Attendance was down, but the animals still needed to get fed.

Then their elephant got pregnant.

Alert ad agency geniuses leapt into action. They put a sonogram of the baby elephant on YouTube. They ran polls and contests (girl or a boy?). Attention was paid. Hoopla was generated. The zoo was back on track, and attendance climbed.

The elephant gave the zoo its mass back. Mass reach, mass excitement, mass crowds. An apparent triumph for new media.

The story is told because it harks back to a happier time, to an era when ad agencies could easily do what they were paid to do: get the attention of the public. It reminds us that our economy is built on the back of mass, on public amusements, on factories organized to create widgets or services or entertainment for anyone (and everyone) with money to spend.

Marketers can be forgiven their nostalgia. Mass is no longer a scalable, predictable way to engage with the public. Success like the zoo's is rare (because pregnant elephants are an oddity). From now on, mass market success will be the exception, the black swan.

Mass is dead. Here comes weird.

Mass, normal, weird & rich

This is a book about four words and how the revolution we're living through demands we change our understanding of what they mean.

MASS is what allowed us to become efficient. Mass marketing and mass production and mass compliance to the rules of society have defined us. Mass is what we call the undifferentiated, the easily reached majority that seeks to conform and survive.

NORMAL is what we call people in the middle. Normal describes and catalogs the defining characteristics of the masses. Normal is localized— being a vegetarian is weird in Kansas but normal in Mumbai. What's normal here is not what's normal there. Finding and amplifying normal is essential to anyone who traffics in mass. Over time, marketers have made normal a moral and cultural standard, not just a statistical one.

WEIRD are what we call people who aren't normal. Your appearance or physical affect might be unusual by nature or by birth, but, like me, you're probably mostly weird by choice. Different by nature isn't your choice, and it's not my focus here. Weird by choice, on the other hand, flies in the face of the culture of mass and the checklist of normal. I'm interested in this sort of weird, people who have chosen to avoid conforming to the masses, at least in some parts of their lives.

RICH is my word for someone who can afford to make choices, who has enough resources to do more than merely survive. You don't need a private plane to be rich, but you do need enough time and food and health and access to be able to interact with the market for stuff and for ideas.

The swami I met in a small village in India is rich. Not because he has a fancy house or a car (he doesn't). He's rich because he can make choices and he can make an impact on his tribe. Not just choices about what to buy, but choices about how to live.

• • •

Human beings prefer to organize in tribes, into groups of people who share a leader or a culture or a definition of normal. And the digital revolution has enabled and amplified these tribes, leaving us with millions of silos, groups of people who respect and admire and support choices that outsiders happily consider weird, but that those of us in the tribe realize are normal (*our* normal).

My argument is that the choice to push all of us toward a universal normal merely to help sell more junk to the masses is both inefficient and wrong. The opportunity of our time is to support the weird, to sell to the weird and, if you wish, to become weird.

The battle of our time

It's not between men and women...

or the left and the right...

or even between the Yankees and the Red Sox.

The epic battle of our generation is between the status quo of mass and the never-ceasing tide of weird.

It's difficult to not pick sides. Either you'll want to spend your time and effort betting on mass and the status quo—and trying to earn your spot in this crowded mob—or you'll abandon that quest and realize that there are better opportunities and more growth if you market to and lead the weird.

Two decisions you'll need to make within the hour:

1. Do you want to create for and market to and embrace the fast-increasing population that isn't normal? In other words, which side are you on—fighting for the status quo or rooting for weird?

   and

2. Are you confident enough to encourage people to do what's right and useful and joyful, as opposed to what the system has always told them they have to do? Should we make our own choices and let others make theirs?

PART 1: CAPITALISM, INDUSTRY AND THE POWER OF MASS—AND ITS INEVITABLE DECLINE

It's not an accident that our instincts, expectations and biases are organized around honoring the masses. We shun the outliers, train students to conform and reward companies that create historically efficient mass market products.

The mass market redefines normal

The mass market—which made average products for average people—was invented by organizations that needed to keep their factories and systems running efficiently.

Stop for a second and think about the backwards nature of that sentence.

The factory came first. It led to the mass market. Not the other way around.

Governments went first, because it's easier to dominate and to maintain order if you can legislate and control conformity. Marketers, though, took this concept and ran with it.

The typical institution (an insurance company, a record label, a bed factory) just couldn't afford mass customization, couldn't afford to make a different product for every user. The mindset was: This is the Eagles' next record. We need to make it a record that the masses will buy, because otherwise it won't be a hit and the masses will buy something else.

This assumption seems obvious—so obvious that you probably never realized that it is built into everything we do. The mass market is efficient and profitable, and we live in it. It determines not just what we buy, but what we want, how we measure others, how we vote, how we have kids, and how we go to war. It's all built on this idea that everyone is the same, at least when it comes to marketing (and marketing is everywhere, isn't it?).

Marketers concluded that the more the market conformed to the tight definition of mass, the more money they would make. Why bother making products for left-handed people if you can figure out how to get left-handed people to buy what you're already making? Why offer respectful choice when you can make more money from forced compliance and social pressure?

Mass wasn't always here. In 1918, there were two thousand car companies active in the United States. In 1925, the most popular saddle maker in this country probably had .0001% market share. The idea of mass was hardly even a dream for the producer of just about any object.

At its heyday, on the other hand, Heinz could expect that more than 70 percent of the households in the U.S. had a bottle of their ketchup in the fridge, and Microsoft knew that every single company in the Fortune 500 was using their software, usually on every single personal computer and server in the company.

Is it any wonder that market-leading organizations fear the weird?

The End of Mass

This is a manifesto about the end of the mass market. About the end of mass politics, mass production, mass retailing, and even mass education.

The defining idea of the twentieth century, more than any other, was mass.

Mass gave us efficiency and productivity, making us (some people) rich. Mass gave us huge nations, giving us (some people) power. Mass allowed powerful people to influence millions, giving us (some people) control.

And now mass is dying.

We see it fighting back, clawing to control conversations and commerce and politics. But it will fail; it must. The tide has turned, and mass as the engine of our culture is gone forever.

That idea may make you uncomfortable. If your work revolves around finding the masses, creating for the masses, or selling to the masses, this change is very threatening. Some of us, though, view it as the opportunity of a lifetime. The end of mass is not the end of the world, but it is a massive change, and this manifesto will help you think through the opportunity it represents.

Weird isn't just the new normal; it's actually a good thing

My ulterior motive in bringing you this manifesto has little to do with helping you sell more stuff and more to do with allowing us (all of us) to embrace the freedom we have. The freedom to choose. The freedom to choose to be weird.

Wholesale compliance, like mass, is a relatively new phenomenon. We're coming to the end of a century of industrialism, a century when manufacturing, marketing, politics, and social systems were all in alignment, all organized to push us toward the center.

The way of the world is now more information, more choice, more freedom, and more interaction. And yes, more weird.

• • •

Welcome to Normal

Take Route 55 south from Chicago. Travel 127 miles and you'll come to Normal, Illinois.

There's a Biaggi's, a Subway, and a Pizza Hut—the usual list of chain joints. Normal is not the sort of place you'd drive out of your way to visit for dinner.

Normal is a fine city, with good people. But Normal is not a fine dining hub; what's more, it's not a strategy, and it's not a reflection on who we are or where we're going.

We're not normal. We're weird. All of us.

Welcome to weird

I'm standing at the corner of First Avenue and 8th Street in Manhattan. Is there a more vibrant commercial corner in New York?

Look, there's the Islamic cultural center across the street, right next to the Atomic Wings buffalo chicken wings joint. Around the corner is Veniero's, a fabled Italian bakery. I can see a group of twenty Chinese tourists out front, just hanging out. Behind me is Momofuku, a modern take on the traditional Japanese noodle bar, run by a Korean chef who grew up in Virginia. Crossing the street is a rich uptown lawyer walking hand-in-hand with a tattooed downtown kid (or maybe it's a tattooed lawyer and a well-dressed tourist). The sidewalk is so crowded you have to stand in the street if you want to stand still.

I haven't even mentioned the place selling hydroponic herbs, the guy who sells fresh bulbs of turmeric, or the Nuyorican Poets Café, where poets, famous and unknown, come to jam while the owner heckles from the back. There are gluten-free bakeries, extra-gluten bakeries, vegan bakeries, and probably a few people selling hash brownies as well.

There's nothing going on around me that would be considered normal by a time-traveling visitor from 1965 (except maybe the brownies). Instead, there are collisions of ideas and cultures and concepts, all unexpected, often filled with positive energy.

And back to normal

About fifty blocks from this little corner in the East Village is the epicenter of New York City's high-rent tourist-based commerce. The Abercrombie store is on Fifth Avenue, right across the street from Tiffany's.

Both stores have lines of tourists waiting to enter. Both sell precisely the same stuff you can easily buy online. And both are cranking out piles of money, selling expensive trinkets, in volume, to people in search of an experience and a souvenir. We've trained people to associate that trinket with a lifestyle, with the attainment of an elite status. Congratulations, you're on the top of the mass heap.

For fifty years, this attainment of mass has been the goal of just about every American business: average products for average people, sold at a high price, in volume. It's been communicated relentlessly to consumers as well—that being the top of the center was where you would be if you tried hard enough. The rule was simple: if you can get the masses to yearn for what you offer, and you can satisfy their needs in bulk, you win.

"He can't be a man 'cause he doesn't smoke, the same cigarettes as me"

Sounds like the work of a marketer, no? Keith and Mick were surely poking fun at the Mad Men and the merchants of mass, at those who understood how to plant the seeds of normal.

This is precisely what marketers were seeking. In trying to build the biggest possible audience, they worked hard to have us ostracize people who weren't as normal as we were.

What does normal mean?

It turns out that statisticians are pretty serious about normal. Consider, for example, the height of adult men in the United States. According to Wikipedia:

> *In probability theory, the normal (or Gaussian) distribution is a continuous probability distribution... the average height for adult men in the United States is about 70 inches, with a standard deviation of around 3 inches. This means that most men (about 68 percent, assuming a normal distribution) have a height within 3 inches of the mean, one standard deviation.*

So, if you're between 5 feet 7 inches and 6 feet 1 inch tall, someone in stats class would say you're within a standard deviation of the mean. In English class, we'd say you're normal.

The average doesn't always matter as much as the *variation* from that average. If your feet are in two buckets and the average temperature of the water is 90 degrees, you're probably fine—unless one bucket is at 35 and the other is at 145 degrees. On average, you're fine. Based on variation, though, you're miserable.

This discussion would be nothing but semantics, except that the variation of the population is changing, and fast.

No, not the variation of height among American men. But yes, just about everything that *is* under our control, everything we get to decide about. We're stretching our behavior outside of that first standard deviation, destroying the 68 percent hump.

Everything that's not normal is weird, and right now, there's more weirdness than ever. Is that a bad thing?

Weird (not normal) means that you've made a choice, that you've stood up for what you believe in and done what you want, not what the marketer wants. More and more, that's precisely what's happening.

What does weird mean?

In this manifesto, I'm not talking about weird by birth, I'm talking about people who are making an affirmative choice to be weird. Most people who make that choice are paradoxically looking to be accepted. Not by everyone, of course, but by their tribe, by people they admire and hope to be respected by.

The weird aren't loners. They're not alone, either. The weird are weird because they've foregone the comfort and efficiency of mass and instead they're forming smaller groups, groups where their weirdness is actually expected.

The key element of being weird is this: you insist on making a choice.

The death of mass media, right before our eyes

Eric Schmidt, the former CEO of Google estimates that every two days, Earthlings produce as much information as was produced by all of mankind for the 20,000 years leading up to 2003. It's not all good information, sure, but there's a lot of it and it can't help but be not-so-normal.

In the lifetime of a typical thirty-year-old American, she has seen the market share (the number of eyeballs watching) of the big three TV networks go from 90 percent to less than 30 percent. In one generation. Pop record sales have gone from a million copies a week to just 43,000 in twenty years. More choice, less mass.

Combine the impact of infinite information creation combined with the dissolution of truly mass media. The overlapping influence of these two trends makes it easy to see that a foundational principle at the core of our culture has just disappeared. Boom, it's gone.

It's like a snowball running downhill, getting bigger and faster. Just when we expect it to get bigger still, though, it splits into millions of smaller snowballs.

PART 2: THE FOUR FORCES FOR WEIRD

All elements of society have shifted profoundly in my lifetime. Almost all of them have shifted in one direction—away from normal and directly toward weird. Here are four of the most significant factors that are changing what we do and what we are willing to accept.

Force one: Creation is amplified.

Publish a book or sell a painting or customize your car or design a house—whatever your passion, it's easier to do it, it's faster to do it, and it's more likely that (part of) the world will notice what you do. The ability to reach and change those around you has been changed forever by the connections of the Internet and the fact that anyone, anywhere can publish to the world.

Force two: Rich allows us to do what we want, and we want to be weird.

Only wealthy organisms are able to culturally diversify, and as human beings get richer and richer, our instinct is to get ever more weird. As productivity has skyrocketed, so has our ability to do what we'd like instead of merely focusing on survival.

Standing out takes time, money, and confidence. More of us have all three now.

Force three: Marketing is far more efficient at reaching the weird.

The long tail isn't just a clever phrase; it's an accurate description of the market for just about everything.

It's easier than ever to reach particular pockets of weird people with stuff they're obsessed with. That makes it far easier to be obsessed, because marketers are willing to go along with your desires, instead of forcing you to do only what they want.

Don't underestimate the power of marketing to make things happen. The fact that some marketers are enabling weirdness is a significant force in the way we act.

Force four: Tribes are better connected.

Because you can find others who share your interests, weird is perversely becoming more normal, at least in the small tribes that we're now congregating in. The community you choose can be a mirror and an amplifier, furthering your interests and encouraging you to push ever further. The Internet connects and protects the weird by connecting and amplifying their tribes.

The historical trend toward mass vs. the new trend toward weird

Here's that conflict again. The thing that made us rich was our ability to process in mass, produce in mass, ship in mass, and market in mass. The advances in productivity were largely about large-scale innovations in production and delivery. Consider nylon, say, or the interstate highway system.

This wealth, though, is fueling a movement that undermines the foundation that earned us the wealth. We needed a mass audience to leverage the assembly line, and the assembly line was supported by TV ads, but as the marketers and factory owners got wealthy, that wealth made the market wealthy enough to no longer sit still and obediently do what we're told to do, undermining the very system that created the wealth in the first place.

Which is fine, because the next breakthroughs in our productivity and growth aren't going to be about fueling mass. They're going to be relentlessly focused on amplifying the weird.

At the same time, marketers of all stripes have eased up on the pressure to fit in. Social structures have shifted and the heroism of outliers has been celebrated again and again. McCarthyism faded and Arlo Guthrie stepped in.

Antelopes don't have hobbies

You need to be rich to be weird.

Not Rockefeller rich, of course, but rich enough to not worry about surviving. Rich enough to care about choice.

Most animals aren't rich. Ever. They forage or hunt, and if they don't succeed (daily), they die.

Human beings, on the other hand, have figured out how to be productive. And as we've gotten more productive over time, our weirdness has followed. Pre-historic cultures, not nearly as productive as ours, show little evidence of the weirdness our culture has recently developed.

Consider the cave paintings in Chauvet in southwest France. 17,000 years ago, human beings became rich enough to paint. That meant that someone was given weeks off from the work of hunting or foraging to spend his time painting instead. It means that the community took the time to make brushes and paints and to admire his work. Few of us would consider this group of cavemen to be rich, but compared to every other organism before them, they were. They were making choices.

Fast forward... compare that one French cave painting to the explosion of work on display at the Museum of Modern Art in New York. There's an almost endless array of subject, medium and approach, all created in the last century. It's not a discussion of better or worse—it's about variety. And variety often comes only if there's wealth. For 17,000 years, we've been on a productivity binge, creating ever more efficiency and value and yes, wealth. Art at the edges is no longer an oddity, it's the norm.

The truly poor don't get to say, "I don't like vanilla, I want chocolate." Rich people, a group that is more and more of the planet, are now expected to say just that. Despite the growing gulf between what politicians label as rich and poor, in much of the world even the poor are rich enough to make choices, rich enough to have passions, rich enough to care about what they watch or what they eat.

When people are truly poor, "Take it or leave it" is an appropriate marketing strategy. Poor means no choice, so the provider gets to choose. Commodities were the best you were going to get, so marketing was primarily limited to "here, want some?" If all you can afford is beans and rice, then beans and rice is all you get. Not a lot of room for initiative or anything we might call weird.

One of the most exciting changes in the way aid flows from the richest countries is that we're realizing that even the disadvantaged want choices, that even people we label as "poor" want control over what they do and how they do it. When we give people choice, we make them richer.

Many who work in international development are quick to agree that people in the developing world deserve choice and want choice, but their actions belie this. The easiest knee jerk reaction is for the wealthy to decide what's needed, and ship it out in a giant container or dispense it from the back of a truck.

Over and over, we see that when you give people a choice, they take it.

Weird as an expression of being human

The marketplace isn't merely about turning a profit. Adam Smith might have embraced the market because capitalism leads to productivity, but that's only part of it. The market also encourages personal choice and engagement. It enables us to be weird if we choose to, not merely to be the compliant masses, waiting for a handout.

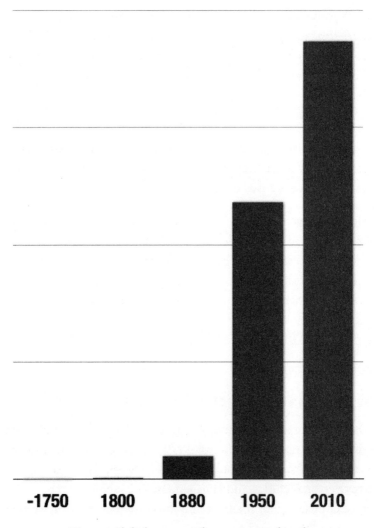

How much light you get for a minute of work

Matt Ridley reported on how much time (or work, or money, same thing) it cost us to buy light, a fundamental building block of our civilization. Twenty-two hundred years ago, you would need to work fifty hours to buy an hour of light from a sesame oil lantern. Today, you can buy an hour of clean, bright light in about *half a second*.

The rapid increase in the availability of things we now take for granted—food, transportation, shelter—means that the world has gotten richer at an astonishingly fast rate of speed. Now that most of us can buy survival without spending the whole day working, we're left to figure out how to spend the rest of our time and money, and marketers are building ever more ways for us to choose.

Often, when we talk about helping poor communities, we're actually working not to save a life but to offer more choices. That's how we improve our well-being—by enabling choice.

Today, there are people who can make a living as painters or professional bowlers or even poets. There are 10 million households with a net worth of over a million dollars. And there are millions (perhaps a billion) people who make enough money from their day job that they're able to pursue something they enjoy with their spare time. More and more often, the thing they enjoy is something weird. Choice is what we choose.

Wealth compounds, and that brings more weirdness

Visit Etsy.com and you can buy a typewriter, rebuilt by hand, that has a USB cable coming out of the back. It'll cost you about $400 to be able to type a novel on your iPad using a fifty-year-old typewriter. The market (and our newfound wealth) enabled Jack Zylkin to embrace his hobby, and it allows you to own something no mass marketer would ever consider making.

For just a hundred dollars more than that, anyone can buy a month-long JetBlue travel pass. Here's what you get: hundreds of planes, hand-built in Seattle or France, staffed by thousands of trained pilots and flight attendants, maintained by thousands of mechanics, controlled by computers (at a cost of billions of dollars of research and development), all standing by, waiting for you to decide where to go. And then they'll take you there, safely. And you can do it again tomorrow.

Any city you want. Every day.

We're surrounded by miracles, by leverage and by the choices created by 10,000 years of increasing productivity. Is it any wonder we're now spoiled for choice, that we expect it, that we demand it?

Productivity compounds. Right now, we gain wealth from inventions made a hundred years ago, discoveries that our parents or grandparents made, shortcuts that were discovered long before we got to work. The ever more networked nature of our world means that we have huge assets at our disposal—laser cutters, roadways, chemical compounds, and innovative ways of processing ideas— all standing by, waiting for us to do something new.

A computer should cost a billion dollars. Instead, you can buy one for $200. The reason? The insights and investments and innovations of a decade or two ago have already been paid for. We get the benefit of the innovations that came before, but we don't have to pay for them—not just the advancements in manufacturing, but those in our networks, in our markets, and in the way various media leverage what we create.

The demand for normal (fueled by the explosion of our productivity since the industrial revolution hit its stride in 1920) is now ironically and inevitably clashing with the trend toward weird (fueled by the explosion of manufacturing and marketing productivity since 1920).

Making an impact on our own culture

Without special training or permission, people can design a T-shirt, throw a party, sing a song, or write a poem. That's not news—these aren't technical skills, they are cultural ones. Human beings have always been creators. We express ourselves, connect with people, and make our home in the world through the culture we participate in.

The biggest cultural shift that the Internet has amplified is the ability to make an impact on your own culture. It's easier than it has ever been to make a video or spread an idea or live your life surrounded by like-minded people. And those like-minded people, when exposed to the poke of your creativity, poke back. New culture is created on top of the old one, and then another layer of culture goes on top of that.

The Pro-Am revolution—the increasing impact of amateurs working to professional standards—means that amateurs, unannointed by any official entity, can publish, create, and connect. It means that a single individual can change the way we think about just-in-time manufacturing, Halloween costumes, or anything in between.

Pro-Am contributors do professional quality work with significant impact, and they do it for fun. They might be discovering asteroids, editing encyclopedias or writing printer drivers for operating systems. Because they can. And the system both enables their work to be of professional quality and leverages it to have significant impact.

The effortless connection of tribes (people who share a culture) reinforces ideas that might otherwise end up abandoned. Tribes with pro-am members accelerate nascent ideas and spread them in a feedback loop that encourages ever more creation.

Stop for a second and consider that this was impossible forty years ago. Impossible. The chance that a typical citizen could create a story, a picture, a device or an algorithm that would change the conversation was vanishingly small. Today, the path from idea to conversation to choice is far more clear. The open door is an invitation that reinforces the impulse to create.

Consider the tragic case of Van Gogh. He sold only one painting in his lifetime, and he lived in isolation, sure that his work was being (and always would be) shunned. Imagine the impact on his life and art if he had been connected to a burgeoning circle of fans and fellow artists.

When an artist (not just a painter, but anyone creating new ideas and new work) is able to have his work amplified, it changes him and also raises the bar for those that would follow.

Post a video of yourself playing Steve Winwood riffs on the twelve-string guitar and you'll hear back from other guitarists within an hour. You've been connected. You see their work, you incorporate it in yours, and you've been amplified.

The Pew Internet and American Life Project reports on the habits of millions of internet users. According to the report, "Many enjoy the social dimensions of involvement, but what they really want is to have impact. Most have felt proud of a group they belong to in the past year and just under half say they accomplished something they couldn't have accomplished on their own."

Chris Anderson of TED has spoken about how rapidly skills as diverse as skateboarding and public speaking have advanced. Artists, performers and geniuses of all kinds can post their work online, see how others improve it, and then raise their game in return.

One result is a rapid increase in the pace of creative development. Jokes and memes and images and inventions and ideas spread faster and farther than ever before, gaining both speed and valuable edits as they travel. And then they come back to us, bringing connection and support with them.

Five hundred years ago, the Portuguese government made it a crime to publish a map of the New World or their other imperialistic explorations. They didn't want anyone to see what was out there. The Web and the tribes it supports are violating that law. Everyone keeps publishing detailed maps so other explorers can go ever faster.

When you don't feel alone, it's easier to be weird, which sort of flies in the face of our expectation that the weird individual is also a loner. Social acceptance of weird behavior makes being weird more popular. This reinforcing effect causes tribes to rapidly splinter off from the now fading idea of mass. The weird person seems normal to her small group of fellow choicemakers, but no, that behavior is not big enough to be attractive to the mass marketer.

As a result, the mass marketer keeps missing the point. He's busy looking for giant clumps instead of organizing to service and work with smaller tribes. Probably worth slowing down and reading that sentence again, because our bias for mass is so strong and so ingrained that we often overlook it.

Smart marketers are already supporting those that wish to choose

Our culture, particularly in the United States, is still about buying stuff. And weird would go only so far as a cultural force here if there weren't souvenirs and junk to buy to fuel our weirdness. Without stuff to buy to support our passions, I fear that many of our passions would fade.

Never fear. Marketers have shifted gears and are leading the push to weird. The smart ones are in fact co-marketing with parts of the market instead of marketing at the masses.

No matter what your predilection or passion, marketers are now able to sell to you and are interested in doing so. Disney will help you get married in Orlando. Zappos will sell you precisely the shoe you have in mind, in whatever size you desire. NetJets will have a private jet waiting to take your CEO wherever he wants to go on an hour's notice. We're so used to having choices, it's almost shocking when we don't have them: what do you mean, no one makes x-c ski boots in wide sizes?

Threadless goes much further than this. They have no art department to design their T-shirts. Their customers design them, and then sell them to their other customers. Want a T-shirt featuring "The Eating Habits of Bears"? They'll happily sell it to you.

In addition to being able to *make* what the market desires, this new breed of marketers are also far better at figuring out *what* the market desires. And as they identify and connect with these non-mass pockets of interest, they're encouraging further weirdness from whatever niche they are in.

If you want to sell $900 handmade rifles to obsessive collectors, the easiest way to grow your sales is to grow the market of obsessive rifle collectors. That means that marketers evangelize this particular weirdness to those who might be entranced by it. And then, as the market grows, they go further, pushing the envelope, making ever lighter and more desired rifles... which means further pushing the edge of what it means to be obsessed. More choices, less mass.

The cycle continues, with the nascent spark of weirdness being noticed and then fanned by the marketers, who in turn hand it back to the market, who get weirder still, further pushing the marketers along the path.

Stereophile magazine runs ads for 3-meter-long speaker cables that cost $1000 per meter (that's for a pair, sure, but still). Those ads pay for the magazine, a magazine filled with articles about weird audiophiles and their silly expensive hobby. Those articles encourage readers to push the hobby further, and manufacturers respond by making ever sillier products.

This cycle leads to the used-goods market, a place like audiogon. com, where less well-heeled but just as passionately weird listeners can buy and sell used gear for half the price of new. Even better, they can find discussion boards where they can discuss, for example, this online post:

> *Connect the primary (high side) leads to an audio oscillator or function generator. These are the blue and brown leads for a push-pull transformer, or blue and red for a single ended one. Set the frequency to 1000 cycles per second and the output to maximum. Now use an AC voltmeter to read the voltage on both the primary (high side) and the secondary (low side). Divide the larger number by the smaller one and square the result. This is the impedance ratio.*

Or consider this one, from a forum about a conversation few of us can imagine being involved in:

> *Dislocation Meshing is a new and promising approach to automatic hexahedral meshing for FEA. The goal of the group is to exchange knowledge, experience and insight on how Dislocation Meshing can solve the practical problems of today and tomorrow.*

Tribes are better connected

Just as marketers have actively worked to amplify the feedback loop that makes weird more accepted, individuals are doing the same thing, even when money doesn't change hands. The reason that people are walking away from mass is not so that they can buy more stuff. Material goods and commerce are not the goal, they are merely a consequence. The goal is connection.

Go to a Tea Party rally and you're more likely to move further from the political mainstream and into the mainstream of the Tea Party instead. Visit a website about extreme tattoo art and you're more likely to get more ink. Attend a conference on just-in-time manufacturing theory and you're more likely to push your company to go ever faster.

Obvious? Of course it is. But it's only in the last few decades that these connection tools have become both ubiquitous and efficient, and the move toward multiple silos instead one giant community is accelerating fast.

One hundred and forty-one brave firefighters in Barbados belong to the Bajan firefighters group on Ning. This online community connects them and reassures them that they are normal in their weirdness. They're obsessed about their craft, and they want to do it right. Not right by our standards (most of us don't understand why someone would spend 80 hours a week risking one's life for free) but by the standards of the community of firefighters.

These communities are each their own silo, each a micro-culture that embraces the original weird notion and then drifts off in its own direction.

Amplified creation, marketing efficiency and the support of tribes, then, are pushing toward one outcome: we're getting weirder. Mass is withering. The only things pushing against this trend are the factory mindset and the cultural bias toward compliance.

We can argue about whether the loss of a cultural center is a good thing or not, but it really doesn't matter what one generation believes is good for the next... all of our choices are leading in just one direction, which is away from the center.

PART 3: THE GRADUAL AND INEXORABLE SPREAD OF THE BELL CURVE

Mass is about the center, the big, fat, juicy addressable center. Governments and marketers and teachers have organized around servicing and profiting from mass. And now, the center is melting.

The (brief) history of fishing

I wonder who it was... the first guy (I'm sure it was a guy) who fished for fun.

Surely, fishing wasn't a hobby three thousand years ago. Fishing was work. Somewhere along the way, though, we got rich enough that we could do things that used to be work—and throw back what we caught.

Wait, it gets even more odd.

While wealth permitted us to find expensive, time-consuming hobbies like fishing, we were pushed to whatever hobby we chose in the traditional way, where 'traditional' was defined by those in power.

Media and marketers ensured that most people would do fishing (this new hobby) the same way as everyone else. *Field and Stream* and other magazines taught hobbyists the 'right' way to do things. Manufacturers encouraged everyone to find a mainstream hobby and buy mainstream supplies. The local sporting goods store sold mass-market items to do the hobby of your choice, but sold only the standard items.

It's really quite recently that it took less than ten seconds to find the $3,500 Orvis Special Edition Mitey Mite Bamboo Fly Rod, or to engage with Rocky Ford's website, where you can find Al Troth's Elk Hair Caddis Olive fly for ninety-nine cents. Now, there are as many sorts of fishing techniques as there are fisherman—and plenty of eager supporters for whatever it is you'd like to do.

And a history of bread

For 5,000 years, if you wanted bread, you baked it. You baked it the way your mother did, from local ingredients, probably including whole grains. It wasn't pretty, but perhaps it was good.

Industrialization gave us the bakery and then the baking factory and then Wonder Bread. Wonder is white, refined, pure and always the same. Wonder is average bread for average people, advertised and promoted and homogenized. Wonder is the regular kind.

In less than a century, we went from a culture of personal to one of industrialization—mass ruled.

And then, of course, Wonder's parent company went bankrupt, the ads went away and the curve spread out. The regular kind isn't necessarily average bread for average people any longer.

For example, Daniel Leader runs a bakery called Bread Alone, earning millions of dollars selling everything but Wonder-style bread. He sells organic breads and spelt breads and sourdough breads and sunflower breads as well. Not just to tiny niche markets but to tens of thousands of otherwise normal people who shop at farmers' markets and are taking advantage of the ability to choose.

There isn't an industrial baking facility in the USA that can afford to ignore the fringe any longer. The center is hollowing out and the fringe is becoming the driving force of what bakers make and what we eat.

We're all edge cases: Kung Fu Fighting

Your music collection is like no one else's. Your visit to the endless buffet line of music now brings back an assortment of songs unlike the assortment chosen by anyone else. What makes consumption interesting—what we seek out, what we travel for or talk about— is not abundance, but the so-called niche items instead.

Why pick one source of music instead of another? For the edgy stuff.

Cory Doctorow explains the popularity of file-shared music thusly: "Why did Napster captivate so many of us? Not because it could get us the top-40 tracks that we could hear just by snapping on the radio: it was because 80 percent of the music ever recorded wasn't available for sale anywhere in the world, and in that 80 percent were all the songs that had ever touched us, all the earworms that had been lodged in our hindbrains, all the stuff that made us smile when we heard it."

In other words, it wasn't the Beatles that made file sharing popular (everyone who loved the Beatles already owned the CDs). No, it was Kung Fu Fighting and the Partridge Family and Sister Sledge that got people hunting for mp3s. We got off the couch in search of the obscure music that wasn't already in the dorm room.

The calculus has been fundamentally and permanently altered: You succeed by fueling and feeding the things we used to call niches, not by enforcing normalcy, however you define it. Tower Records couldn't satisfy our endless desire for variety and they disappeared.

The bell curve is spreading

The distribution of a population is often shaped like a bell curve. For example, if you asked all the kids in a school to line up in order of height, the graph of how many kids were of each height would be shaped like the classic bell—you'd have as many 4 foot kids as 6 foot kids, and a whole bunch more in the middle at 5 feet.

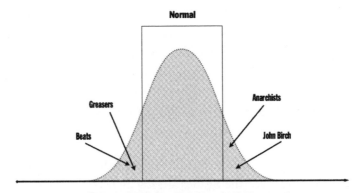

In 1955, the distribution of behaviors was tightly grouped

Not surprisingly, this curve is called a normal distribution. It's incredibly common in almost any phenomenon you look at (Internet usage, miles commuted to work, length of hair).

Something surprising is happening, though. The defenders of mass and normalcy and compliance are discovering that many of the bell curves that describe our behavior are spreading out.

The bell isn't gone, but it's different

Marketers were amazed and delighted to have a century in which not only were the markets they sold to defined in fairly easily found bells, but the bells were also tight. Almost everyone would drink a Pepsi or a Coke. Almost everyone would wear Keds. Almost everyone would speak English.

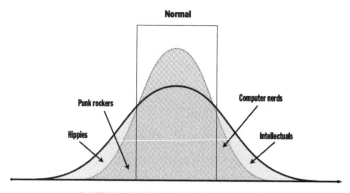

In 1975, the distribution of behaviors was spreading

Running a cafeteria was easy because everyone ate the same thing. Running a travel agency was easy because everyone wanted to go to the same places.

Distributions of behavior remain, but as the anchors holding that behavior in place have loosened, the bells have spread, like a thawing ice sculpture.

The number-one brand of rice in the supermarket used to be Carolina. Now it's "other." Corn Flakes used to account for most of the cereal shelf—now that shelf at the superstore is longer than the entire packaged-foods section of the market was a few decades earlier.

Cars used to come in just black, then a few colors, and now Scion sells a car deliberately designed to be repainted, jacked up, and customized. We want what we want.

You can argue against this trend at your peril. There are few marketers, politicians, religious leaders, or parents who are able to successfully push back against this oozing.

It started with ice cream

The idea of thirty-one flavors of ice cream is ridiculous. So is a wine store with five thousand varieties at two hundred price points. So is the notion of the Thomas Register, a multi-volume book listing every supplier and vendor eager to sell businesses the tools they need to make anything, from a device that will scan your peanut brittle assembly line for little bits of metal to a conveyor belt system that's 3 percent faster than the one you have now.

Of course, the decay of limited choice and the compliant masses didn't start with ice cream. The road to weird started with the royal court and the printing press and the capitalist's desire to find a niche without easy substitutes. As soon as merchants discovered they could make a profit by being different, they began to work at being different.

This trend was compounded by the birth of the industrial age. If you're a manufacturer, you don't merely desire specialization, you insist on it. If a new part or a new consultant or a new process is going to improve your productivity, you'll buy it.

There has always been choice for those who could afford to choose. Now, though, more and more of us (perhaps 4 billion) can afford to make choices. People we used to assume were too poor to matter, too poor to deserve a choice or earn market power, discover that they too can choose.

Power to the chooser

A few kilometers outside of Berelli, India, in a tiny village where the average person makes $3 a day, I sat with a fruit vendor talking about his new solar lantern.

He *chose* the lantern. He bought it. It wasn't given to him by the manufacturer or an international aid organization. He picked it because he wanted it, because, according to his calculus, it was worth it. That means D-light, the lantern's manufacturer, has to figure out how to delight people like him if it wants to gain more customers.

This man, a person we could have easily written off as poor, is now rich. He's not rich because he has everything he wants and needs—far from it. No, he's rich because he can make a choice, rich because he is part of the marketplace, one that cares about what he's interested in.

When you can add people who make just a few dollars a day to the list of people entitled to choice, you've opened the door to half the world.

The marketplace brings power to the chooser

Not all hedge fund operators are the same, and neither are all rural peasants. Any system that treats them as homogeneous groups is taking away their ability to be individuals. Mass marketing had little choice but to do just that, because there wasn't an effective way to reach just the few customers who might be interested.

The marketplace, though, can no longer act with the blindness of marketers. If people choose to interact, they gain power, because their choice is up to them, not the marketer. If you want me to buy from you, perhaps you should acknowledge and then respect my weirdness.

On one hand, we celebrate choice. We want choice and we imagine that others would, too. No one says that it's morally wrong to prefer chocolate over vanilla, or that it's selfish to be a vegetarian. At the same time, though, organizations and producers are seriously threatened by choice, they fear weirdness, and they push us to fit in.

As soon as consumers enter the marketplace, they gain power, because power comes from choice. Consumer power is a brand new force, and it's growing exponentially as a result of more affluence running in parallel with more choice.

Many bell curves, not just one

Forty years ago, it wasn't unusual for bestselling books to stay on the list for a year. Movies might dominate for months at a time.

Back then, we spent a lot of time trying to read what everyone else was reading, watch what everyone else was watching.

Now, a bestseller is a hit for only a week or two, and then there's another one. The reason is that instead of just one list, we're seeing many bestseller lists laid one on another. One tribe after another nominates a hit. A rap song and then a ballad. A thriller and then a comedy. A book for thirty-year-old geeks and then one for moms.

Many bell curves, not just one. We don't care so much about everyone; we care about us—where us is our people, our tribe, our interest group, our weirdness—not the anonymous masses.

Mass is to us as water is to a goldfish

We've been living with the assumption of mass for so long, we don't even notice that the assumption that everything must be normal is so deeply ingrained. It's ingrained in the mom who buys her kid normal layette clothing so both of them will fit in. And it's ingrained in the kid who is told he can't wear his Batman cape to school, because the other kids don't. And it's ingrained in the high school senior who gets sick on beer in order to fit in with the brainwashed group of his peers who think that doing what all the advertising has been selling them is cool indeed.

We've been trained since birth to enforce the status quo. Our bias is to the *many*. To please the many. To sell to the many. To be organized to serve the many. We admire politicians based on how many votes they get from the many, we listen to Top 40 radio to hear what the many are also listening to. Our armed forces are filled with the many, fighting the many, on behalf of the many.

Corporations choose accounting firms based on the many. Cafeterias cater to the many, as do the highways we build and the medicines we invest in.

Surprise. The weird are now more important than the many, because the weird are the many.

The Mad Men Mass Premium

Why are brands like Seven Up, Nationwide Insurance, Alka Seltzer and Tide so valuable?

The answer is easily overlooked: For more than forty years TV ads were too cheap.

TV delivered mass to marketers. Buy enough ads and you bought trust. Trust and shelf space. The combination got you not just sales today, but sales tomorrow.

For three generations, TV generated significantly more in value than it cost the advertisers. The ads didn't have to be great, or even good. Brands merely needed to run a lot of them. The surprising thing is that relatively few marketers understood this, so the number of uber-brands is not nearly as large as it might have been. It took guts to spend all your available cash on TV ads, and few took the risk.

The result of this extraordinary discount: some marketers got hooked on mass. They got addicted to the notion that they could grow and profit and make the quarterly numbers by creating average products for average people and advertising them a lot.

And then it stopped working. Quite suddenly, TV splintered and suddenly it wasn't such a screaming bargain. Suddenly, the maxim, "Spend every penny you can," didn't work anymore.

Which leaves thousands of TV addicts, brands with nowhere to turn, stranded without a plan.

They're addicted to mass and there's no mass available.

Tom Harrison runs the DAS group at Omnicom, the second-largest ad agency holding company in the world. Here's the surprising thing: Tom's group, which contains all the non-advertising parts of the company, all the publicity, promotional and service components, has grown from 11% to nearly 60% of the company's revenue in less than fifteen years.

That's right, more than half the revenue at the second-largest ad agency in the world comes from activities that aren't mass advertising. Game over.

Whom shall we disappoint?

Perhaps the most difficult (and often least productive) meetings that mass marketers have are about alienating groups of customers or vendors.

If you persist in trying to be all things to all people, you will fail. The only alternative, then, is to be something important to a few people.

And to get there? To get there you must disappoint some slightly engaged normal folks, who, to tell the truth, can probably live just fine without you.

The ski area at Jackson Hole has a choice: to become even more welcoming to extreme skiers who seek out the expert trails, or to dumb the facility down to be more open to the average skiers who represent the bulk of vacationing travelers who might consider a trip.

You can probably hear the argument in your head. "But if we don't open more beginner slopes and build a new lodge, we'll lose these customers to Aspen!" It's not easy to walk away from average, because average represents mass, or the promise of mass. The chance to become the next Wonder Bread/Budweiser/Chevy is seductive, but no longer practical. The field is too crowded, and there's not enough upside after you build a middle-of-the-road normal brand.

If you cater to the normal, you will disappoint the weird. And as the world gets weirder, that's a dumb strategy.

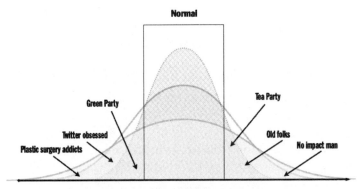

By 2010, the distribution of behaviors had spread to the point where there was more weird outside the box than normal inside it.

The Gutenberg parenthesis

Researchers at the University of Southern Denmark have pointed out that the five hundred years of the Gutenberg revolution are drawing to a close, that even something as apparently stable as the mass-marketed book is not going to be around much longer.

The ability for billions of people to create and spread their own version of the culture is something brand new, something that will make the changes of the last decade look trivial.

The opportunity lies in being the one that the weird seek out. Which means you must be weird as well.

Johnny Carson wasn't weird

In 1972, *The Tonight Show* was watched by twice as many people as the 2010 versions of *Late Night* and *Leno* combined. Every night.

We pretend that what's on network TV matters when it comes to reaching the masses. It doesn't. That's because there are fewer masses.

The Beverly Hillbillies has been replaced by *Mad Men*. You can be a TV critic if you want, but the marketer in you needs to acknowledge that fifteen times as many people watched Jed Clampett as watch Don Draper.

Does the opportunity to grab the middle even exist for you any longer?

You haven't seen everything

Anil Dash points out that there is no longer a canon—no longer a corpus of work that a culturally intelligent person could be counted on to have experienced. It's possible to have never seen *Star Wars* or attentively listened to Beethoven being played live. It's possible to not know the significance of Keith Hernandez or Keith Moon or Keith Olbermann.

Making it worse, the endless varieties, remixes, and spin-offs mean that even if you have experienced one version of part of the canon, there's another better faster different version that only the obsessives have interacted with. I own more than fifty versions of the Dead singing *He's Gone*, and I haven't even made a dent.

This explosion of choice and variation has a significant cultural impact. It sets us free to spin and gambol at random, getting weirder at every turn because once you're a little out of sync, there's little reason to avoid getting a little more out of sync.

How many billion?

McKinsey advisor and Harvard Professor Eric Beinhocker calculates that there are 10 billion items for sale in New York City alone. That's up from two hundred items about five hundred years ago.

As soon as the numbers start with a "b," they're too big to count, too big to store, too big to corner the market on.

Ten billion items, all vying for our attention, all shouting for a sale, all sitting, just waiting to get picked. Can we agree that almost everything on this endless list is weird?

Digital is not a shadow, it's a light (start with the 'Net)

The interconnected nature of the Internet (more than one in twelve of the people on the planet use Facebook) has gone beyond the sideshow of the dot-com boom and ended up influencing everything that's made and sold and distributed and discussed.

It used to be possible (even advantageous) to ignore the digital hoopla. Focus on your work and who cares whether Oprah is on Twitter. Now, though, it's basically impossible to interact with the future (or the present) without determining how digital interactions are going to change the game.

Even if you're a sod farmer in Georgia, the price of your supplies, the market for your goods, the availability of your workforce— it's all being manipulated digitally, long before you enter the picture.

The Internet encourages weirdness for two key reasons:

1. It's a private connection between one person and another, and occasionally public, instead of a public broadcast that's occasionally private. You can be weird on your own long before the "culture" (what's left of it) tells you to stop.

2. There are a billion "channels" of information and you can pick the one you want. There's a long tail of channels, and at least one matches every person's precise definition of weirdness (if there's no match, go ahead and start another channel).

The result of this is a cycle that encourages customized, optimized interactions that push people to be individuals, not to fit in.

Physical proximity as a barrier to weird

Teenagers frequently complain that there's nothing to do in town. No one to see, no one to talk to.

Online, there's always something to do.

For centuries, we were limited by geography. The things we could buy, churches we could join, languages we could learn, music we could hear, foods we could eat—all of it was gated by what was physically available. You could run with the "bad crowd," but only if you could find them.

Today, of course, it all comes to you with a click.

You can go on a raw food diet without living near a health food store. You can join the Zoroastrians without living in India. You can support a political party with no activists in your neighborhood.

As soon as we remove physical proximity as a gating factor, the only barrier to weirdness is choice.

We're already used to the bell curve

Smart marketers have never treated the market (any market) as just one market. Instead, it's well understood (thanks to Everett Rogers and others) that the market has geeks, nerds, early adopters, laggards, and the mass in the middle.

As you think about the inevitable fragmentation and spread of mass, it's worth a minute to consider again how the product adoption lifecycle works.

I like to use the market for video as an easy way to visualize this lifecycle. On the left, in the small lead-up to the hump are the early adopters. These are the folks who watch all their video on an iPad. They used to use Tivo, but that's old-fashioned.

In the center, the hump consists of those using a DVD player they bought at Walmart for $80. And to the right, the laggards. They're the ones who still have a 12:00 flashing on their VCR.

When a new entity, like Netflix on Demand, comes along, it often works its way through the curve. The first users were video geeks, or techno geeks, or people looking for a cool toy. They told their friends, the ones who are too busy (or so they think) to pay attention to new stuff. If it's great, they use it, too.

Worth noting that the two groups are looking for different benefits. The nerds define "great" as being new and interesting and somehow noteworthy. Their friends in the center, though, define "great" as something that is cheaper, faster, and reliable.

The laggards, of course, just wait until what they have breaks, and then, with no choice, reluctantly begin using something a bit newer.

Now, as the curve spreads, the geeks are even geekier. They don't want the new thing; they want the beta version. They don't want the thing that's new; they want the thing that's so new that the other geeks don't even know about it. And a geek with an eye for denim might be specializing—denim isn't enough, it has to be selvedge denim, or even better, selvedge denim from Japan.

Are any of these little micro-segments big enough to make a living on? Possibly not. As the market gets increasingly addressable and non-anonymous, though, the efficiency gained more than makes up for the small size of the market. Instead of reaching 5 percent of the geeks in your segment, the combination of permission marketing and the connections of tribes might permit you to reach 20 percent. The market might be far more specialized (and thus smaller), but your share is bigger.

Stuff is not the point

So much of marketing and culture is about consumption, because that's where the money is. We measure, tweak and improve the way we buy and sell, because that's all in a good day's work, at least in a society where money is the thing we measure and try to grow.

But consumption is not why we're here, consumption is not the point. The very same dynamic that is changing the world of marketing is changing the way we govern ourselves, raise our families and take care of our health. The bell curve (and its spread) has an impact on our ideas and our culture, regardless of whether we are buying, selling or merely living.

The key lesson: humanity and connection are trumping the desire for corporate scale.

The objects far away may appear more normal than they actually are

When we see a jogger off in the distance, our brain fills in the gaps. We don't imagine a red-haired giant, wearing a chartreuse jumpsuit and a Cameron Diaz smile. No, at this distance, we fill in the gaps with our prototype runner, a standard runner, the runner we always use when we imagine a runner. To do anything else seems a waste of time and effort.

As we get closer, reality intrudes. This isn't an archetype, it's an actual person. Short, perhaps, or with just one leg, or limping or wearing street clothes. On close inspection, just about everybody is weird.

And that's the key: *on close inspection.* The reality of digital community is that people are now available for close inspection, and the 'Net allows us to keep all of them in focus at once.

Since we don't need the shorthand of archetypes and standards and straw men, we have no choice but to accept the truth of weirdness.

Average is for marketers who don't have enough information to be accurate.

The forces for normal

- Big media
- Manufacturers
- Franchises
- Large service firms
- Many organized religions
- Politicians
- Law enforcement
- Shipping companies

There are countless exceptions, primarily among outliers that have chosen to cater to the weird. But the fact is, many organizations that seek to dominate their market would prefer it if we would just go along with the plan.

Apple is happiest when everyone (everyone) wants to buy a new model iPod. The TSA is happiest when everyone (everyone) is willing and able to follow all of their instructions. The IRS would prefer it if your taxes fit on the 1040EZ form and took just a few minutes to process. And you can bet that big mass-market advertisers and ABC would be delighted if everyone would just settle down and watch the same show at the same time.

I've started using the word "factory" to define any organizational effort that's built around repeated interactions and mass. If you need a map and a manual, it's probably because you're creating a business or a campaign that's based on a factory. If exceptions are a problem, it's probably because you're doing factory work. Most of all, if you're focused on hiring down, on finding compliant cheap workers, then you're running a factory.

Factories have their place. They generate things like a reliable Holiday Inn experience, or a flight that lands on time or a DVD player that costs $30 and works every time.

But factories don't like weirdness. The challenge, then, is to figure out which side you're on.

Three (new) forces for weird

- Explosion of wealth
- Explosion in media choices
- Explosion in shopping choices

That's it. That's enough.

We've been so immersed in media that we forget how much it has pervaded our existence.

The Internet takes the impact of media and magnifies it. (The Internet is the first medium that not only pokes you but makes it easy to poke back.)

We engage with the Internet at work, we wear it on our hip, we check it at soccer games. All media, all the time—just not the media that the mass-media people were hoping for.

And then there's Google and the redefinition of shopping. It didn't use to be possible (never mind easy) to shop for latex lingerie, free-lance copy editors, or a wine store down the street from your client in Florida. It didn't make sense to compare the pricing on business card printing—it just wasn't worth your time.

Now, we can find it. And if we can find it, we can buy it, pray to it, interact with it, argue with it, share it, and get involved with it. Whatever *it* is.

Even better, we can make it ourselves. We can make our own books, photo albums, and software. We can spec a 3D object and print it on our desk, or ship it electronically to a factory that will churn it out.

The forces of normal have no clue how to defeat this me-ness, this shrine to our weirdness. They're going to try, but it's hard to see how that's a side worth betting on.

Two hotels

My friend Chip started a string of hotels in the San Francisco area. Starting twenty-five years ago, each hotel was personal and authentic—and different. You would walk into a hotel and say, "wow, this is me, this place is about me." Or perhaps you'd say, "what the hell is this?"

The details were right. The Phoenix was in San Francisco's bad neighborhood, and it wasn't even a hotel. It was a motel, with a hand-painted swimming pool and parties all night. It was Linda Ronstadt's favorite place—she booked the entire hotel for her band when her tour came to town.

As the boutique hotel trend morphed and grew, some of the mass market hoteliers (like Hyatt) took a look and said, "Well, these are cheap hotels with relatively high prices. Let's knock some off and fleece a new part of the mass market." After all, they can skip the tub, the shaving mirror, the expensive desk, the in-house laundry.

I'm writing this from the desk in my room at the Andaz Hotel in Los Angeles, Hyatt's attempt to get weird. Except it's not weird, at least not to me. It's *not quite right.*

The Beatles album framed on the wall is a little too predictable. The little eraser that has the word "oops" printed on it. The too-clever pad of paper that was designed by a committee, not by a person who cares. It's the work of a mass marketer trying to pander to the edge, instead of someone edgy talking to people in his tribe. And it doesn't work.

It doesn't work because while they did the surface things, the easy things, the cheap things, they failed to do the hard work of being (and embracing) weird. It's sort of weird for the masses, not the work of an actual human being with interests. There are no risks here. There's no humanity, either. Even the people who work at the desk are following a script, *pretending* to be weird, they're not one of us, the truly weird, the hip outliers the hotel is trying to attract.

The paradox is that these masses that Hyatt is shooting for, the ones who would prefer fake weird to real weird—they're not going to stay here, either; they're not going to talk about it or seek it out. No, they prefer real normal, not fake normal.

As choice and self-determination continue to triumph, you can't profit from it by *pretending* you're not a mass marketer. You actually have to *stop being* a mass marketer.

Harry Potter and the conflicted masses

Harry Potter movies always open at #1, the most popular film in the United States. And many people go for precisely that reason. They belong to the mass tribe, to "everyone."

Deep down, many of us enjoy doing what other people are doing.

This is why fashion works. Why there are pop songs. Why every company in the *Fortune* 500 uses similar HR policies. It feels good to be part of the herd.

Except...

Except when it doesn't. Except when we'd rather see a foreign film or eat raw fish or institute a ROWE system at the office.

Hence the conflict.

For a long time, mass marketers held the upper hand. The big studios controlled the theaters, for example, and a hit movie might run for three months. With no cineplexes and no Blockbuster, you saw what was playing or you saw nothing at all.

The mass market myth is crumbling. As a result, we seek out the rare global hit with a nostalgic kumbaya. We watch the Super Bowl, not so much for the game as to remind us what it was like when all we did was what everyone else was doing.

It's true that we want to be part of a tribe. What's not true is that it must be the uber tribe, the one and only mass tribe, the center of the curve. Our own little circle is in fact what we really want.

Mobile is as weird as media gets

Mass media comprised three channels of TV. Odds were you could reach everyone.

Cable splintered this into twenty or thirty or forty silos.

The Web went a step further. Now there are a billion websites, along with asynchronous interactions like e-mail.

But mobile is the weirdest of all. That's because in addition to the silo of me (just me), I add time (I want it now or I want it never) and location (I want it here or I don't want it). The urgent uptake of mobile devices is further proof that individuals want to connect with their tribe (their Facebook friends, their Foursquare circle, their frequently texted buddies) far more than they want to interact with the more average (more normal) world. Mobile rewards right here, right now, all about me thinking, which is anathema to the factory-based marketer in search of mass.

Since each market is now a market of one and a market of now, the marketer has no choice but to surrender all pretense to mass.

If I'm standing on the corner of Houston and Greene Street at three o'clock in the afternoon, what I want, right there, right then, is the only media I am willing to consume. Don't talk to me about a special offer at The Gap or a way to lower my company's workers' comp expenses. No, I just want to know where to get some chocolate sorbet in the next three minutes.

You can reject that idea as too weird or you can work with me (and the billion other weird people like me that aren't quite like me). Up to you.

Jenss and the three suits

When I was thirteen, I needed a suit. I was twenty pounds over-weight, and I was short for my age.

The only place in Buffalo to buy a suit was Jenss. I honestly have no recollection of where anyone else in my town got office or party wear, but as far as I knew, it was Jenss or nowhere.

"We have three suits in your size," my mom and I were told. The ugly one, the uglier one, and the one that didn't fit.

"They are just not showing suits in your style or size now."

I have no idea who "they" were. I knew that there wasn't a Brooks Brothers or a Men's Warehouse or a Syms or a Macy's to visit. Three suits, and *they* weren't interested in making one I would enjoy wearing.

The reasoning was rational, even if I didn't like it: It only made sense to cater to the middle of the market. It was too risky and too expensive to create suits for short chubby kids. Why bother? It's not like there were many other places vying for my business.

As fresh as this memory is for me, today it's laughable. In any place with a mall (or an Internet connection), the number of choices approaches infinity. There are polyester suits with vests that would look at home in a *Superfly* movie; there are bespoke handmade suits from Mexico for $350 and even cheaper ones from Thailand.

If you've got only one leg, you can buy a single shoe from Nordstrom's online. They'll take care of finding a home for the other half of the pair.

An explosion of supply, an explosion of retailers, and a brutal battle for market share have caused "they" to rethink what the market looks like. What they've figured out is that mass, the middle of the curve, is nice work if you can get it, but the few customers left in the middle are not enough. There are too many edge cases missing now.

T.G.I. Friday's comes to Union Square (the struggle between mass and weird)

Union Square in New York is where money meets weird. It's the home of the largest greenmarket in New York, the most popular restaurant in Zagat's, and an ever changing array of public art exhibits. It also used to be the home of Zen Palate, an unquestionably small chain of vegan Chinese restaurants.

The rent got too high, Zen Palate couldn't cut it, and they were replaced by an avatar of chain sameness, T.G.I. Friday's.

Apparently, weird isn't enough. Not this time.

Scarce real estate supports normal. In a battle between someone fighting for the edge and someone picking up the remains of mass in the middle, the middle will win if there's room for only one.

The change: real estate matters less. Scarcity matters less. Choice matters more.

In the world outside of real estate, there's room for more than one.

The middle is splintering and then re-splintering. No one has the mass they want to have, and in the long tail world of choice, this means that those brave enough to seek weird will thrive.

The ebb and flow of weird and normal

Normal begets normal. As totalitarian regimes of government or brands or even the organizations of society begin to gain power, they demand more compliance. Those who are in the tribe of normal understand that their power will increase if they can push others to comply as well.

As the population gets more compliant, those in charge gain power. Factories find that they can eke more productivity from workers who do what they're told, and marketers enjoy the benefits of being able to predict how the masses will respond.

And so the powerful spend money and media and authority to ensure compliance, until it approaches its maximum.

Then an interesting thing happens—pockets of people discover that they can gain power and increase joy by being weird. So they splinter off. They spray graffiti on the wall or start their own projects or speak up.

And weird begets weird.

The weird set an example for the rest of us. They raise the bar; they show us through their actions that in fact we're wired to do the new, not to comply with someone a thousand miles away.

That's where we are as a culture right now—on the up part of the curve. No doubt there will be bumps along the way. A shock, an incident, a revolution will occur and we'll momentarily become sheep again. But I can't help but think that it won't be for long.

TV vs. Boing Boing

Mass-market TV has a real estate problem. There are only a few channels, so, like the landlord in Union Square that sold out to a chain, network TV sells out to mass, every time.

Even cable TV demands huge silos. The Food Channel is happy to broadcast only TV about food, but it works hard to cater to the masses of that audience, not the edges. Most of all, they seek out comfort, offering something that is like it was yesterday and will be tomorrow, because they don't want to lose the very tenuous hold they have on an audience (and advertisers) that they've lulled into a sense of security.

There's a reason ESPN always seems the same. The sport may change, the people might change, but when you watch the network, you're home.

That's why Americans watch thirty-four hours of television a week. We're pacifying ourselves with mass.

Visit any expat hotel in a far-off locale. There will be a bar, and behind the bar you'll see a TV. Odds are, it's playing ESPN and there are dozens of people eagerly watching. This is what homesickness looks like for many—the comfort of seeing familiar figures playing a familiar game.

Boingboing.net, a website founded by Mark Frauenfelder, takes a different tack. If it's weird, they want it. If it's different, that's good. If it's new, that's good. If it might fail, that's good.

Ten minutes on Boing Boing reminds me that the world is changing, moving, and getting weirder. It eggs me on. Ten minutes of ESPN puts me to sleep.

One is for creators and the other is for those seeking safety (and nostalgia), at least in the moment.

(And worth noting: ten years ago, ESPN was considered a flaky outlier, not the place you'd invest your ad dollars. The middle continues to fade.)

Mass and the reign of a normal education

Seen from a distance, everything looks about the same. If you have to educate 4 million new students every year, you really have no choice but to see them at a distance. Up close is too close to see them all.

It's understandable that school administrators and textbook authors and boards and Regents and admissions officers and the rest of the education-industrial complex are a bit overwhelmed. They deal with this by optimizing for normal. They step far, far away so they can get a good look at all the students they have to serve.

Normal is the pretty cheerleader with good grades and just enough extracurricular activities to seem well-rounded. Normal is the popular football player who defines who is in the In crowd, and who shows up in class enough to not set a bad example (but who sneers at the idea of giving up time with his friends in order to score great grades). Normal is the normal kid who does what he's told, studies hard, and takes his studies seriously (this kid is fictional).

We compare the other kids to the normal ones. The closer you get to the normal ideal, we say, the less pressure we will put on you to conform. We organize our teachers and our classes and our systems around this normal. Sure, we make allowances for the really smart ones (the abnormally smart, the ones who get special classes, a shout out at graduation, and an invitation to MIT) and the disabled (who are ignored, or tracked, or once in a while, while we pat ourselves on the back, mainstreamed).

The normal education system takes precisely twelve years to graduate a normal student from public school. Normal education is built around a standard curriculum, one size must fit all. Get too far ahead and you stress us out—cut it out, kid. Get too far behind and we fail you, reprocess you, give you another chance to get with the program.

Seen from a distance, these 4 million people are in fact mostly normal. Certainly more than half of them are close enough to the center we've defined that we can happily cater to them, reward them, and move them through the system without paying too much attention to who they are or what they need. That frees up the staff to deal with the outliers, the ones who mess up all our efficiencies.

The slow kid, the fast kid, the girl who wants to be on the football team—all of them are exceptions, outliers, weirdnesses to be extinguished.

Corporations, the ones that need workers, try to find the normal ones. It's easier that way. Easier to hire and train the new workers who have always had little trouble fitting in, no trouble following instructions, no issues with doing what they're told.

We encourage kids and parents and teachers and coaches to help us enforce this normal middle. The bullies—the ones who torment the outliers, the gay kids, the dreamers, the math nerds, the visual artists—they're just being kids; *lighten up*. The coaches that bench the students who have more enthusiasm than athletic talent—*try harder, kid*. The teachers who are given classes so big that they have no choice but to focus on the middle, avoiding or failing the kids that don't get it quickly enough.

Education reform, then, tends to focus on raising the standards for the middle. After all, the middle is the reason we started school in the first place: to populate our culture with normal.

The establishment sees this group from a distance, this huge bog of humanity that apparently needs to have its bottom raised. We say we need to fail schools that can't create enough conforming output. We say we need to test students harder, to find out which ones haven't accepted or internalized the learning that's on offer, and thus refine the center, ensuring that the normal ones are as reliable as promised.

And so the factory-for-the-production-of-normal works overtime to sanitize and corporatize and discipline our kids into normalcy.

Seen up close, normal disappears

What great educators have discovered, though, is that there is no blob of normal. There is no center of the curve, no pack of students who have no problems, no talents, no issues. Instead, there are millions of silos, millions of individuals and small groups that learn differently, think differently, and dream differently.

What are we going to do with 4 million weird kids? Every year!

When a six- or seven- or eight-year-old kid is gifted at visual thinking, why do we shut her down and force her to do fractions?

When a teenager wants nothing more than to organize and to solve interesting problems, why do we push him to study for the SAT instead?

When the standard at a school is defined as mediocre, why don't we celebrate and leverage the student who's willing to push the envelope and produce heroic work?

The challenges of the education system are driven by our distance from the problem, not by money. The disconnect is caused by our fervent desire for a return to normal, a normal we actually never had.

Why are we puzzled that in a world filled with change, a static, history-based approach is not working out so well?

Aside: The simple solution to education

A different approach to education is almost impossible to conceptualize and seemingly impossible to execute.

The simple alternative to our broken system of education is to embrace the weird. To abandon normal. To acknowledge that our factories don't need so many cogs, so many compliant workers, so many people willing to work cheap.

It's simple, but it's not easy.

It's not easy because we can't process weird. We can't mass-produce students when we have to work with them one at a time or in like-minded groups. We can't test these kids into compliance, and thus we can't have a reliable, process-oriented factory mindset for the business of education.

No, it's not easy at all.

When we consider whom we pay the most, whom we seek to hire, whom we applaud, follow, and emulate, these grown-ups are the outliers, the weird ones. Did they get there by being normal students in school and then magically transform themselves into Yo-Yo Ma or Richard Branson? Hardly.

The stories of so many outliers are remarkably familiar. They didn't like the conformity forced on them by school. Struggled. Suffered. Survived. And now they're revered.

What happens if our schools (and the people who run them and fund them) stop seeing the mass and start looking for weird? What if they acknowledge that more compliance doesn't make a better school, but merely makes one that's easier to run?

My proposed solution is simple: don't waste a lot of time and money pushing kids in directions they don't want to go. Instead, find out what weirdness they excel at and encourage them to do that. Then get out of the way.

Weirdness and happiness

What has the highest correlation with happiness? Is it wealth? Your astrological sign? How attractive you are?

In fact, Ronald Ingleheart and other researchers report that the ability to be weird, the freedom to make choices, and the ability to be heard are the factors most highly correlated with happiness around the world. Regardless of income or race or geography, when we let people choose among things that are important to them, they become happier. More varieties of jeans doesn't necessarily make people happier, of course, but the opportunity to live where they want, say what they feel, express their desires, and choose a path certainly does.

Weird is everywhere you look

Sometimes, we forget to bother. Sometimes we're not trained to see it.

But it's there, and growing in strength every day.

There are so many

When you watch any form of media, or visit a city, or read the newspaper, it seems as though the number of "others" is a lot higher than it used to be.

Our instinct to get back to normal (our fond memories of a normal that never existed) is a natural response to the widening gyre of weirdness that surrounds us. The myth of sameness that marketers sold us a generation ago is fading. This fraying around the edges increases the desire of tribes to tighten up, to remind themselves of what it means to be normal, to not see the edge of town but to feel as though perhaps everyone is normal, at least for a while.

Some people are more comfortable believing that there are no edges, that everywhere is like it is right here. That they are normal, that everyone is normal, and that ignorance is bliss. If everyone could just be normal (like them), they'd be happier.

This is precisely the opposite of the emotion felt by those who attend the crossword puzzle convention or the women's professional rodeo tour or the Maker Faire. In this case, it's the outliers, the previously alone, who are getting together in order to reinforce their nascent movement. They're well aware that their world doesn't extend forever; in fact, it might not go much further than this tent they're standing in.

In both cases, though, tribal power is being exercised. It's human nature to be weird, but also human to be lonely. This conflict between fitting in and standing out is at the core of who we are.

Tribes are fueled by our never-ending desire to avoid loneliness. Weirdness (which used to be a shortcut to lonely) is now fueled by the very tribes that fought it.

The weird have an obligation, too

If marketers are going to cater to the edge cases, then the edge cases have to step up and spend money, speak up and get involved. Yes, they have to act a little less weird, and organize into tribes willing to engage with the outside world.

If you want there to be interesting new plays on Broadway, you need to buy a ticket when they arrive, even if the next play is not a crowd-pleasing Tony winner. If you want marketers to make exactly what you want, you have to tell the marketers what you want. And then keep your promise and buy something when they make it.

The reason that classical music is endangered is simple: people who say they love classical music stopped buying tickets and records. We're left with nothing but Beethoven's greatest hits because the people who could show up and represent the edges would rather whine than show up.

On the other end of the cultural spectrum, there's an endless parade of new tech devices because tech nerds buy them. If you organize and amplify your tribe, the marketers will notice.

Consumers have more power than ever before. What a shame it would be if all we used it for was to get a Whopper for a few pennies less.

The morality of weird

Morality is a tricky topic, one that you might be surprised to find in a book about marketing and the way society is changing.

While we as humans generally agree about the core principles of morality (don't kill people, don't steal, don't hit your little brother even if your parents aren't looking), it turns out that there are many other areas in which there's not a lot of agreement.

Where did these other rules come from? Do we all agree on the answers to these questions?

Is it immoral to charge interest on a loan? Read a particular book? Eat a certain kind of fish or meat? Is it immoral to marry someone of a certain caste or ethnicity?

In previous books, I've written about the power of tribes to influence our lives. Tribes are groups of people aligned around an idea, a community, and a mission. These tribes need leaders, and those who lead often get hooked on the power that comes with the job.

One way to strengthen and maintain a tribe is to demand conformity. If all the people wear the same hat or speak the same language or perform the same rites, the tribe gains power. Union solidarity isn't just a slogan; it's actually the most effective tactic for workers facing a powerful boss running the only factory in town.

In many cases, we enforce this compliance by building a religion on top of the tribe. A religion as a set of rules and promises and benefits, a religion as a cultural artifact. For example, vegans have a religion, and a key tenet is that you don't eat fish. If you do, you're doing something wrong and you've violated the trust of the rest of the tribe.

The intersections between power, tribes, and compliance suddenly get very interesting. If a nascent leader creates a schism and walks off with a splinter group, his power over this group is enhanced. If I can tell you that some other group is wrong—not just different, but wrong—then I increase my power over you.

Humans have an ingrained need to do the right thing. We succeed as a civilization because we're wired to be open to morality, to avoid being desensitized selfish entities. Marketers and leaders often take advantage of that openness to create new standards that feel to us like moral imperatives.

In other words, we believe it's moral to comply.

Or at least it seems that way.

Whenever significant weirdness shows up in society, defenders of the status quo speak up to decry the *immorality* of it. Freeing the slaves was decried as immoral. So was female suffrage, as well as the movement for women to work outside the home.

Generations later, most of us have come to the conclusion that precisely the opposite is true, at least for these issues, and that the new normal (the weird) is also the new moral.

When people in power tell other people what to do with their hobbies, their work, their passion, and their lives, we run the risk of enforcing the status quo by pretending we're talking about morality when we're actually using fear or corporate greed as a motivator.

Hence the stress that so many organized religions face today. When the religion ceases to be about faith and hope and connection and love and positive change and begins to focus on compliance, this organizational embrace of the status quo runs straight into the trend toward the weird. Playing the morality card is a weak way to build a tribe.

Weird is not immoral.

Ism schism

The easiest way to make noise within a community is to divide the tribe.

Modernism, classicism, realism, impressionism—dividing things into schools of thought, or even warring camps—makes it easy to create tension and thus attention.

Marketers (and organizers, politicians, and manipulators) have discovered that one way to create mass is to define normal as "us" and abnormal as "the other guys." If you can alienate and demonize, then by definition, the remaining group is yours to do with as you choose.

I'm running out of patience for people who would further their personal or media goals by dividing us in exchange for a cheap point or a few votes. If members of a tribe encourage schisms and cheer on the battles, is it any wonder that it's hard to create forward motion? When we're not in sync, power is dissipated.

Intentionally pitting people against one another to generate a mass audience is dangerous self-indulgence, because inevitably the tactic is used again to further split the group.

Consider the benign example of the world of fine art. Once the Impressionists were banned from mainstream art shows in the 1800s, it fueled the power of their movement. As the schools of art continued to morph and split, though, so did the audience for art. Jeff Koons may be making more money than Monet ever did, but his impact on the public is far smaller, and probably always will be because his "public" is a tiny portion of the masses.

Art has, like most things, become weird. Those who pursue their art (or the business of selling it) by pursuing the weird have consistently outperformed those who seek to create mass.

Others (weird)

- Atheists
- Hispanics
- Computer nerds
- Polo players
- Jews
- Paraplegics
- Communists
- Tea Party members
- Native Americans
- Non-English speakers

Are they like you? Are they to be trusted?

When your tribe is no longer the majority, then what?

Origins of dominion

Someone always wants to be in charge.

But how?

The long-term plan is to train people to accept someone giving them orders. Sure, we can resort to physical force, but the arithmetic doesn't support asymmetry. If you need one foreman for every subject, you're not going to be able to scale. And actual restraints and fear for one's physical safety are not effective motivators. Instead, dominators have long created cultural norms that dictate that the lower class (as defined by the upper class) should obey their superiors.

For thousands of years, leaders have enforced their rule by telling us stories and selling us on the idea of compliance.

The stories in all ancient mythologies revolve around powerful gods that told humans what to do—and those gods were ignored at the peril of one's life.

I don't think it's an accident that these stories were invented and then reinforced and amplified by human leaders. They push the population to accept "normal" and they encourage peer pressure to comply. If effective society is defined as people accepting authority, then everyone in the society has an incentive to enforce the rule of just a few.

So emperors and princes and then kings like Louis XIV pushed forward this idea of normal, of being an insider, of doing what you were told.

Marketers, discovering a good thing, joined in. By doing the only commercially viable thing (marketing to the middle of the curve), they unintentionally latched on to this old idea of pushing society to the middle. As democracy created positions of power for the elected, these newly elected leaders did the same thing. They campaigned to the middle and thus had an incentive to push society in their direction.

Today we can see that the post-industrial age and the Internet permit a different sort of power, one of silos and smaller but tighter networks. Now, there's an incentive to fragment instead of coalesce. And given the choice, given the chance to be weird, more and more of us are taking that chance.

Sure, there are traditionalists in the center, ranting and pushing and haranguing society to get back to the good old days, to the days of compliance. There are Supreme Court justices willing to criminalize behaviors they consider weird. There are corporations who fire employees for speaking up. There are dictators who imprison someone worthy of a Nobel Peace Prize.

The reactionaries that demand compliance, though, face an up-hill battle. They will have a hard time becoming Torquemada in Spain, 1492; they will have a hard time enforcing a rigid status quo when ideas are easier to spread, mobility is easier to find, and marketers find profits in niches, not mass. As I review the final draft of this paragraph, I'm watching headlines from Egypt and Libya that remind me once again how hard it is to maintain order if order means, "doing what the dictator says."

Is there any doubt at all that we're going to get weirder?

Girolamo Savonarola and the failed fight for control

In 1497, Savonarola organized the Bonfire of the Vanities. He and his followers went from house to house, seizing items that they said encouraged moral turpitude. Things like mirrors, "pagan" books, gambling sets, dresses, and even chess pieces. They burned them in the town square. Savonarola is even reputed to have personally thrown paintings by Botticelli into the fire.

There will always be small tyrants like this. U.S. Senators who want to execute someone for running a website. School boards that want to install cameras to catch students misbehaving at home.

The progress of our society, though, is relentless. It just keeps getting weirder. The behavior that little men would try to enforce today would have been scandalous just fifty years ago, because the standards keep changing. The markets that seem like big opportunities today were tiny rounding errors a generation ago.

Sure, there are those that demand we obey their particular set of standards, their selfish code of conduct. Me, I'd prefer to bet on freedom. And there are those that seek only to serve the hypothetical masses, the John Q. Public who is precisely in the middle. Me, I'd prefer to bet on weird.

The fact is, some days I don't care about marketing. I don't care so much about whether or not Nike sells another sneaker or Marlboro sells another cigarette. What I care a great deal about, though, is each human's ability to express her art, to develop into the person she is able to become. I care about the connections between people and our ability to challenge and support each other as we create our own versions of art. And I care about freedom, the ability to express yourself until it impinges on someone else's happiness.

All of these arts and freedoms require a society that won't just tolerate weird but will actively applaud it.

It's merely a happy coincidence that we live in a time when smart marketers can also make money doing something we need done anyway.

Stuck on normal

If you've made it to the end of this manifesto and come to the conclusion that you need to spend more time going after niche markets, I fear we have both failed.

Those in power tend to describe the world as us and not-us. White and non-white citizens. Apple products and non-Apple fans. Mass and non-mass (we even made a fancy French name for it: niche).

This will get you only so far, and not very far at that.

The revolution that we're living through has many facets, and a profound and overlooked one is that mass is not the center any longer. Us and not-us is a dead end.

Instead, consider a lens that sees Lisa, Ishita, and Rafit. There is no us. No mass. No center. Our culture is now is a collection of tribes, and each tribe is a community of interests, many of whom get along, some that don't.

We all share communication tools. Most of us share the same three or four languages. We all share the same planet. But we're not the same. We're people with choices, and we won't alter those choices merely because we used to have no choice.

No niches. No mass. Just tribes that care in search of those who would join them or amplify them or yes, sell to them.

This is not utopia, but it is our future.

POSTSCRIPT: ONWARD TOWARD TRIBES

Cindy Gallop's favorite quote is, "Everyone hates advertising in general, but we love advertising in particular."

It's true, of course. We don't like the advertising that's not for us, not about us, not interesting to us. But talk to me, directly to me, about something relevant and personal, and I love you for it.

This goes far beyond advertising and actually informs how we feel about politicians (we hate them, except the ones who are for and about us) and products and causes and government agencies and even birthday parties (those kids at the next table are incredibly annoying, unless they're here for my party...)

The many silos of interest we live with now enable a totally different sort of communication, certainly, but they also demand a fundamentally different sort of organization, one that can deliver *particular* instead of general.

Dishwashing soap is general. Family sedans are general. Coca Cola is general. Please don't dress up your general and pretend it's particular. It's not. When you do that, you're not catering to the weird, you're defending mass in any way you can.

Your policies are general. The way you deal with the public is general. Our knee jerk reaction, inculcated by generations of mass, is to worry about the big hump in the middle of the curve, not to obsess about the weird outliers.

The story of Tom's Shoes is largely misunderstood and worth revisiting. Blake Mycoskie started a shoe company with a simple but radical idea: Every time he sells a pair of shoes, he gives an identical pair to someone in the developing world who has no shoes.

That's it. That's the business model. No ads, no serious promotions, no hype.

Do you see that this has zero in common with the pregnant elephant at the Antwerp Zoo?

Tom's is particular. The elephant is general.

Blake understands that his shoes (and his story) aren't for everyone. In fact, the story of his shoes are for a tightly knit group, a tribe, a group of people who share an interest and a passion and a way of talking to one another. One person rushes to buy his shoes, but then *that* person tells the rest of the tribe, not Blake, not Tom's, not their ads. Tom's is organized around particular. It thrives when someone resonates with its weird story, but most of the time, for most of the world, Tom's is invisible.

This is fine with Blake. And fine with the members of Tom's tribe. It wouldn't, on the other hand, be fine with Pepsi or Taco Bell or Dreamworks. *They're still searching for a pregnant elephant.*

The relentless search to recreate the mass of the past is at the heart of the stress we feel at work. It's pushing governments, NGOs, entrepreneurs and most of all, big marketers, to go to extravagant lengths to push us to conform. A few outliers, though, have seen a different path. They're catering to the weird instead.

The challenge of your future is to do productive and useful work for and by and with the tribe that cares about you. To find and assemble the tribe, to earn their trust, to take them where they want and need to go.

Many marketers would like to become a modern PT Barnum (but with a better circus). That's not the goal, though. The goal is find and organize and cater to and lead a tribe of people, embracing their weirdness, not fighting it.

This single shift in our culture has opened the door for a huge outpouring of creativity, innovation and art. Your turn.

Acknowledgments

Thanks to each Domino for shaking things up and being weird, and proud of it: Lauryn Ballesteros, Willie Jackson.com, Amber Rae, Amy Richards, Alex Miles Younger, Michael Parrish DuDell, and Ishita Gupta. Also great, and weird in a very good way: Lisa DiMona, Lisa Gansky, Jacqueline Novogratz, Faith Salie, Sunny Bates, Sasha Dichter, Jonathan Sackner Bernstein, Alan Webber, William Godin, Nicholas K, Steve Pressfield, Sarah Kay, Sarah Jones, Beth Comstock, Linda Boff, Vicky Griffith, Russ Grandinetti, Amy Bates, Philip Patrick, Kristi Coulter, Sarah Tomashek, Sarah Gelman, Mary Ellen Fullhart, Lynette Mong, Galen Maynard, Alan Turkus, Terry Goodman, Megan Jacobsen, and Jeff Bezos. Always bonus thanks to Catherine E. Oliver, Martha Cleary, Paul Robinson and Red Maxwell.

To Helene, Alex & Mo.—super weird.

About The Domino Project

Books worth buying are books worth sharing. We hope you'll find someone to give this copy to. You can find more about what we're up to at www.thedominoproject.com.

Here are three ways you can spread the ideas in this manifesto:

1. Hold a discussion group in your office. Get people to read the book and come in and argue about it. How open is your company to innovation and failure? What will you do if your competitors get better at it than you are?

2. Give away copies. Lots of them. It turns out that when everyone in a group reads the same thing, conversations go differently.

3. Write the names of some of your peers on the inside back cover of this book (or scrawl them on a Post-it on your Kindle). As each person reads the book, have them scratch off their name and add someone else's.

Tweet your thoughts: #weirdDomino

We hope you'll share.

About the cover

What does it mean to be rich? Or weird?

Pictured on the cover is Jeremy, a competitor from the World Beard and Mustache Competition. He's proudly weird, and rich enough to be able to choose his passion.

It's so easy to look at someone like Jeremy, or at a swami in India or a scuba diver off Belize or at a pack of Santa impersonators in Portland... and call each (or all) of them weird.

"Weird" because they're not like you or, perhaps more urgently, because they're not normal the way a marketer insists they be.

And that's what rich creates. Rich isn't a measure of a bank balance. No, rich means making a choice, choosing an identity and following a path that matters.

Based on that notion, we're at our best when we're weird, and when we're enabling others to become weird as well.

If we're going to demonize, criticize and isolate people who no longer fit our definition of normal, we will fail. The alternative is an attitude based on respect, the respect we accord to someone brave enough to choose precisely what it is they want.